HONOR YOUR WELLBEING

FIONA SEIGNEUR

Copyright © 2018 Fiona Seigneur

Published by DVG STAR PUBLISHING

All rights reserved.

ISBN: 1-912547-16-3
ISBN-13: 978-1-912547-16-6

DEDICATION

This book is dedicated to my two sons; Gentlemen you have always been my rock and reason.

My mother and sister and brother in law, nieces and nephews in Australia and my late Dad let his soul RIP.

My sisters from another mother Jules and Chez AND to you the reader.

ACKNOWLEDGEMENTS

Special thanks to some very special people in my life who I am grateful thankful and blessed to call some my peers and others close friends, in no particular order

- Philip Chan: www.the10-secondsmathsexpert.com
  www.jetsetlearning.com
  www.10secondstochildgenius.co.uk

- Sabrina Ben Salmi and family: All can be found on Facebook, Sabrina is a Mumpreneur, Author, Public Speaker, Business and Personal Development Consultant.

The Fantastic Five:
Lasahi Ben Salmi
Tray-Sean Ben Salmi
Yasmine Ben Salmi
Paolo Ben Salmi
Amire Ben Salmi

- Mark Anthony Clarke- Founder of Walk to Freedom www.walktofreedom.org.uk

- Roxanne and Sheldon St Clair: The Founders of the Value in You
www.thevalueinyou.co.uk

- All the fitfam at local gym Fit4Less Hoddesdon Herts
www.fit4lesshoddesdon.co.uk

- Champions of Mind – Rhys and LLewelyn Davies and James Burtt
www.thechampionsofmind.co.uk

- Professor Chris O'Imafidon - Excellence in Education
www.excellenceineducation.co.uk

- Prasanthika Mihirani of Swiss Graphic Design- Can be found on Facebook
www.swissgraphics.mihiri@gmail.com

- DVG STAR Publishing
www.dvgstar.com

VERY SPECIAL THANKS ALSO GOES TO:

A) Alistair Hesselton
   Twitter@aph_inspired
B) Norma of Norma creates
   www.nomacreates.com
C) Dave Wilkes
   www.justdivinepoems.com
D) Chrissy B
   www.chrissybshow.tv

TESTIMONIALS

...a delightful book full of important reminders which is written to cater to all ages of how to maintain our health and wellbeing and for those who are experiencing a challenge to their mental and or physical wellbeing, it is a compact companion to encourage them to never give up.

Professor Chris O'Imafidon
"Father of Britain's brainiest family, adviser to Governments & Leaders" CNN, BBC, Fox, Sky TV

A heart-felt, wise, honest, and helpful book. Enormously helpful both to those facing low mood and those who just want to maintain excellent health and wellbeing.

Juliette Francois- Assone
CSR Manager at MCB Bank Limited Mauritius

CONTENTS

FOREWORD	1
INTRODUCTION	5
CHAPTER ONE MINDSET MATTERS	9
CHAPTER TWO ANIMAL INSTINCT	23
CHAPTER THREE HAPPY HORMONES	27
CHAPTER FOUR FOODS AS MEDICINE	31
CHAPTER FIVE GETTING BACK ON TRACK	47
CHAPTER SIX GOD TURNED IT AROUND FOR GOOD	57
CHAPTER SEVEN LAUGHTER IS THE BEST MEDICINE	63
CHAPTER EIGHT OXYGEN AND OBSERVE	75
CHAPTER NINE SLEEPING SOUNDLY	81
CHAPTER TEN NOW OVER TO YOU	87
EPILOGUE	91
ABOUT THE AUTHOR	93

FOREWORD

In life there are only 3 certainties:

1- We are born
2- We will one day leave this earth
3- In between there will be days where we all need encouragement due to the uncertainties in life.

We all have goals and aspire to enjoy the life in our years however sometimes in life things will happen beyond our control.

Often it can be a combination of things that happen over time where by someone feels out of control that leads them to feel knocked down completely, fighting to find their balance again.

In Fiona's book, HONOR YOUR WELLBEING, she shares her experience of learning how she had to re learn how to balance the different responsibilities she had thrust upon her and learn again how to HONOR HER WELLBEING after experiencing a low time in her life after experiencing the 5 major losses in life, all one after the other in a short time, ie; Loss of her Marriage, Loss of her Family and Friends Network, Loss of her job, Loss of her late Father and finally the loss of her independence all at the same time as becoming adjusted to life as a single mum in a country she wasn't yet accustomed to and at that time had afforded her little support in raising her two young boys.

How do you cope after such a low period in life?

The key is in your MINDSET and also YOUR ACTIONS.

In this book, Fiona also shares with readers some of her tips and advice not only from her personal experience, however the experience of others also,.

So enjoy Fiona's book HONOR YOUR WELLBEING, the first in a 5 part series of books Fiona has written. I wish you all the success, love and highest wellbeing in every area of your life.

Take new actions and change your thinking, and start learning how to once again, HONOR YOUR WELLBEING.

PHILIP CHAN
10 Second Maths Expert
Award Winning Author
www.jetsetlearning.com

"

Your true success in life begins only when you make the commitment to become excellent at what you do.

Brian Tracy

"

INTRODUCTION

This book has been written as a motivating guide that is aimed to help you or your loved one on your "mental wellness" recovery journey or for anyone that may need some encouragement to improve their health and wellbeing due to stress.

It's my intention to introduce or reinforce strategies that will help you understand what is going on right now and assist you to find a stronger best version of yourself.

Disclaimer:
All strategies shared in this book is intended for use in addition to any GP plans, if you are under a GP.

No claims are being made that these strategies will work for everyone.
I'm grateful though to say they have worked for many so far.

BEST PRACTICE SUGGESTIONS

What would happen if you tried to swallow an apple whole?

In the same way, it is recommended that you read a chapter then take five minutes to complete the various exercises in this book, where included.

Remember, your illness doesn't define you, your strength and your courage does.

"

It's not whether you get knocked down. It's whether you get up.

Vince Lombardi

"

CHAPTER ONE
MINDSET MATTERS

MINDSET MATTERS

In this chapter we will be covering the following topics in regards to mindset:

* What does it take to have a Winning Mindset?
* How do YOU feel right NOW?
* Work/life balance
* What is Seigneur Strategies?

*What does it take to have a Winning Mindset?

According to Michael Jordan, in his own words;

"You will always miss 100% of shots you don't take."

According to Vince Lombardi,

"Winners never quit and quitters never win."

According to Louis Zamperini,

"You don't give up; you fight to the finish."

What do them and their quotes have in common?

Write down your answer below:

_____
_____
_____

If you answered as: their POSITIVE WINNING MINDSET, you are correct.

Life will throw all sorts of challenges and in some cases, constant changes at all of us at some time.

Generally speaking, if it was you that instigated the change, it's easier to adapt.

What if it was an unexpected change and you had little opportunity to deal with it?

What if you kept adding more stresses to life with no break?

It's obvious what would happen, isn't it?

Your MIND and BODY over time would get tired emotionally, physically and spiritually and in time this affects your life financially.

However with the correct winning mindset and actions to counteract, how much of a positive difference that can make?

*How do YOU feel?

If you or your loved one feels tired emotionally, physically and spiritually right now, just know it's OK to admit that this struggle is taking place.

The fact you are reading this book shows, despite all, you are wanting to REGAIN BACK CONTROL of YOUR LIFE.

Whether or not, you recognise it right now, as the great Les Brown says;

"YOU HAVE GREATNESS WITHIN YOU."

YOU are ready to accept that you will never be the same person, however, this gives room for a better you to evolve.

YES, YOU are ready to help yourself **NOW**!
To make the deliberate changes needed to move forward with who **YOU** are to become and ((smile)) again.

***Work life balance?**

I want you to imagine the following scenario;

> A) Moving to another country where the language is the same however the system and culture is very different,

ADD IN…

> B) Raising two young boys, one with Aspergers Syndrome without yet acquiring the full set of skills needed to deal with being his best friend, (which is why I mention it)

THEN ADD IN…..

> C) Managing a full time job or two,

Does it sound like a lot?

In my case it certainly was!

In brief, I had come to the UK for family reasons and had thought it would all just slot into place. I had done the research into the school I wanted my boys to attend and Im grateful that because things always had gone well, it didn't enter my mind that they wouldn't get in.

In addition, little did I know, that in a short period of time, my youngest son, who has aspergers syndrome however wasnt aware of it yet, would come home from school one afternoon sharing with me how he had seen a video at school and as I was already juggling the emotional rollercoaster was unprepared in every way when he demanded to know if he was autistic.

Indeed it was a rollercoaster at that time and the huge move caused a lot more stress than originally anticipated and in addition, I was constantly working 2 or 3 jobs on a temporary basis, to be able to make ends meet and "keep it together" as a single parent until I was made to face the fact, that Wonder Woman is a great film however a myth in reality.

By now you may have guessed, a few years later, due to the stress of it all, I experienced burn out.

I'm extremely grateful beyond words to say my

breakdown, although took time, also became my break through.

I'm also grateful, fast forward another few years, and it also then became the catalyst to the writing of this book and the birth of Seigneur Strategies.

*What is Seigneur Strategies?

What is Seigneur Strategies you may ask?

We are a health and wellbeing company focussed on teaching various strategies for the mental, physical and financial wellbeing of young adults aged 20+, based around what we call the three Ps of great health and wellbeing;

Promotion,
Prevention and
Protection

Through providing workshops with all to do with young adults' wellbeing and individual coaching, initially over a 7 week period, and we also offer other packages that can be located on our website at www.seigneurstrategies.com

BACK TO BALANCE....

Through the traumatic experience described above, I learnt that ALL areas in our lives need to be in **BALANCE.**

These areas are;

A) Work/Career/Business

B) Family

C) Health/Fitness

D) Finances

E) Intimate/Partner Relationships

F) Spiritual/Belief in something bigger than you

G) Friends/Social life

H) Hobbies

This first exercise looks at all of these in detail for yourself. You will need to complete the following chart by circling a score from 1-10 for each area mentioned.

Number 1 being the lowest and reflects the fact that you are not satisfied with where you are in that area and 10 being the highest, reflecting the fact that you are extremely satisfied with where you are in that area..

A) Family
1 2 3 4 5 6 7 8 9 10

B) Health/Fitness
1 2 3 4 5 6 7 8 9 10

C) Finances
1 2 3 4 5 6 7 8 9 10

D) Intimate/Partner Relationships
1 2 3 4 5 6 7 8 9 10

E) Spiritual/Belief in something bigger than you
1 2 3 4 5 6 7 8 9 10

F) Friends/Social life
1 2 3 4 5 6 7 8 9 10

G) Hobbies
1 2 3 4 5 6 7 8 9 10

H) Work/Career/Business
1 2 3 4 5 6 7 8 9 10

Look at areas concerning others, i.e.; A, D and F, and perhaps H also.

How have you scored on these?

Did you know when YOU are under a lot of stress, YOUR BRAIN and MIND can play tricks on you into making you think people don't care. In fact, most times they do care and they miss you, as the person you were prior to what you are experiencing, and not everyone knows how to deal with that.

SO FIGHT BACK BY TAKING CONTROL OF YOUR THOUGHTS.

FURTHER CALL TO ACTION

Looking back at the answers you circled above,

Close your eyes and see yourself in each area where you want to be in and then keep working towards becoming that person daily.

"

There is only one thing that makes a dream impossible to achieve: the fear of failure.

Paulo Coelho

"

CHAPTER TWO
ANIMAL INSTINCT

In this chapter we will be covering the following topics:

*How aware are you of animals 6th sense?
*How can animals help YOU?
*How much has animals played an important role in society?

*How aware are you of animals 6th sense?

Do you remember the Tsunami in 2004 that occurred off the west coast of Sumatra, Indonesia?

In brief, according to Wikipedia, the shock had a moment magnitude of 9.1-9.3, and a rating of "violent". What was noted in the report of the earthquake was the animals in Indonesia prior to the earthquake were seen to be acting strangely.

This was based on an area that was hit by the disaster being an animal reserve that had leopards, elephants, buffaloes and more than 130 species of birds, yet after the disaster, there were hardly any carcasses to be found, according to the facts recorded after.
In fact, BBC reported that

Thirteen countries were affected, the worst being Indonesia, which was hit by the tsunami first. Forty-five minutes later the tsunami reached Thailand.

What happened to all the animals during the Tsunami?

Interestingly, people reported seeing the animals running to higher ground prior to the earthquake.

It's also known that migrating birds such as geese can accurately navigate their way to their destination through the guidance of only the stars and the sun guiding them.

Could it be that animals are endowed with special senses?

Keeping it simple, what about domestic animals? For example, a cat or dog?

How do you think they could help you?

Write your answer below;

----

*How can animals help YOU?

ANSWER:
Let's compare your answers to the ones following;

They can offer tactile benefits in helping you if YOU are experiencing great distress or challenges by:

- Providing you with empowerment as you are their leader/master.
- Offer great companionship
- Giving you accountability and responsibility to care for another,
- Playing with or petting an animal can increase levels of the stress reducing hormone called oxytocin, while also lowering the stress inducing hormone called cortisol.

So if you haven't already, have you thought of obtaining a pet?
YES/NO

What if you are unable to have/house a pet?
Thankfully, this need not be an issue, there are various organisations that employ people to offer owners the service of dog walking, or alternatively you could offer to help a pet owner directly.

CHAPTER THREE
HAPPY HORMONES

In this chapter we will be covering the following topics:

*What are endorphins?
*How are endorphins released?
*Benefits of exercise at all ages

***What are Endorphins?**

The layperson calls it 'Happy Hormones', but what are they and how do they work?
According to the English Oxford Dictionary:

"The term endorphin relates to; a group of hormones secreted within the brain and nervous system and having a number of physiological functions.

They are peptides (A compound consisting of two or more amino acids linked in a chain) which activate the body's opiate receptors, causing an analgesic effect.ie; drug relating to relieve pain."

Are you aware that the human body produces at least 20 different endorphins?

These are produced by the central nervous system and can create a natural high.

At time of writing this, not all of the roles endorphins play in the body are understood fully.

What is known is that, these "neurochemicals" (technical term) acts on the part of YOUR brain that reduce pain and boost pleasure, resulting in a feeling of wellbeing. What is also known is that these endorphins are released in response to;

- sex
- exercise
- laughter and even just
- stretching your body daily

These are just to name a few.

***Benefits of exercise at any age**

When you read the word exercise, what came to your mind?

A gymnasium filled with people lifting heavy weights or aerobic classes with men and women in leotards and leg warmers?

Well, maybe not that extreme, however, just to clarify, exercise can be done anywhere.

If you have stairs indoors, you can practice climbing them at least twice a day.

If you find it a challenge to get out of bed right now, what about reaching over and touching your toes?

YES, even though you find it a great effort right now,

KEEP DOING IT, ANYWAY, EVERY DAY because small positive steps repeated consistently over time CAN and DO yield big results.

CHAPTER FOUR
FOODS AS MEDICINE

In this chapter we will be discussing the following topics:

*What are Superfoods?
*Who is Nomacreates?
*How can YOU get started?

***What are Superfoods?**

Look at each of the foods below in the left column and match them to the column on the right according to what YOU think the body organ that the food is good for.

A good tip is to think of the actual food mentioned and ask yourself what part of the human body it most looks like. The first one has been completed for you.

Answers can be found at the end of this chapter.

Foods	Good For
Tomatoes	Heart
Celery	Eyes
Carrots	Bone
Walnuts	Kidney
Kidney Beans	Brain

The foods listed above in the right column are known as **Superfoods** but what are Superfoods?

The Oxford Dictionary defines a Superfood as food considered especially nutritious or otherwise beneficial to our health and wellbeing.

This is to say that the food you and I eat are used to give us energy, and protect us from illness and general disease. Superfoods are foods that do this at a higher level than others.

At its basic level, it incorporates many fresh ingredients, rather than processed and contribute to a healthier life and better wellbeing.

Some of these foods are plant based and can help YOU when you are experiencing fatigue, stress and or early depression. There are also specific Superfoods for different distinct benefits.

For example, foods rich in magnesium and calcium help your body to get a good night's sleep and include foods such as walnuts, spinach, and kale and almonds.

Just ask my mum, she worked in Medicine for many years and taught me much about Superfoods growing up, although at that time, their benefits were known, however I wasn't aware of the label **Superfoods.**

*Who is Nomacreates?

I am grateful and thankful to have got together with an award winning nutritionist, Nomalanga Nyamayaro, who has a BSc Honours degree in Food & Nutrition and is a BBC One MasterChef Quarter Finalist (2016) to also confirm the validity of these Superfoods today.

I also requested of her a 7 day menu plan for your starting point, to assist you in bringing these foods into your own diet.

Monday

Breakfast

- ✓ Glass of lemon infused water or Pomegranate juice OR
Chamomile Tea

- ✓ Avocado sliced on rye bread drizzled with basil infused olive oil.

Lunch

- ✓ Jasmine rice with green lentils and kale.

Dinner

- ✓ Roasted butternut squash stuffed with a mixed vegetable quinoa.

Tuesday

Breakfast

- ✓ Lemon infused water
- ✓ Blueberry and apple smoothie and
- ✓ 5 seeded bread with pumpkin, sunflower and flaxseed.

Lunch

- ✓ Warm courgette salad with cherry tomatoes and red onions.

Dinner

- ✓ Coconut creamy spinach, with butternut squash and wild mushrooms, served with brown rice or quinoa.

Wednesday

Breakfast

- ✓ Lemon infused water/Chamomile Tea OR Raspberry and Blueberry Smoothie

Lunch

- ✓ Honey drizzled Banana slices with soya yoghurt topped with pumpkin seeds.

Dinner

- ✓ Fish curry with grilled aubergine served with brown rice.

Thursday

Breakfast

- ✓ Lemon infused water/Chamomile Tea
- ✓ Melon and watermelon fruit salad topped with fresh mint

Lunch

- ✓ Noma's Creates African Rainbow salad
- ✓ Lentil soup with rye bread

Dinner

- ✓ Shredded red cabbage with coriander, stir fried in a fennel infused oil.
- ✓ Served with couscous.

Friday

Breakfast

- ✓ Lemon infused water/ Chamomile Tea
- ✓ Spinach & courgette with spring onion omelette.

Lunch

- ✓ Smoked mackerel served with a warm kale and butternut squash salad.

Dinner

- ✓ Steamed cassava with kale and a red onion & tomato warm salad.

Saturday

Breakfast

- ✓ Lemon infused water/Chamomile Tea
- ✓ Oatmeal pancakes topped with raspberries and a spoon of soya vanilla Yogurt.

Lunch

- ✓ Homemade Guacamole served on pumpkin seed crackers.

Dinner

- ✓ Pan fried salmon with sautéed broccoli and green beans served with crushed potatoes drizzled with basil infused oil.

Sunday

YOUR TREAT DAY

Breakfast

- ✓ Papaya, mango and banana smoothie.
- ✓ Herbal Drink of your choice
- ✓ Sour Dough Toast with condiment of your choice. / Cereal/

Lunch

- ✓ Drink of your choice
- ✓ Fettucine with Broccoli and chicken.

Dinner

- ✓ Warm courgette ribbon salad drizzled with parsley and chive dressing with baked lemon & garlic seabass, served with roasted potatoes.

Start to include one Superfood ingredient a day to begin with, then slowly keep building it up to become part of your meals every day.

ANSWERS TO THE SUPERFOODS QUIZ

Tomatoes → Heart

Celery → Bones

Carrots → Eyes

Walnuts → Brain

Kidney Beans → Kidney

"

I learned that courage was not the absence of fear, but the triumph over it. The brave man is not he who does not feel afraid, but he who conquers that fear.

Nelson Mandela

"

CHAPTER FIVE
GETTING BACK ON TRACK

In this chapter we will be covering the following:

*Who is Alistair Hesselton?
*What can you take from his story?
*Now back to you

*Who is Alistair Hesselton?

Alistair Hesselton played football at Premier League level for Liverpool. He was 23 years-old when he was catapulted out of the windscreen of a car driven by Wingate & Finchley FC team-mate, Simon Patterson, as it smashed into barriers on the A40 in London, in the early hours of September 10, 2006.

Alistair's team mate, Patterson, died at the scene, while Hesselton was thrown from the car, and landed on his head in the road, fracturing his skull and leaving him in a coma.

Doctors thought Hesselton would suffer severe brain damage and would probably never play football again.

However, he left hospital, just a few weeks after the crash, and has since represented his country at the Paralympics with the Great Britain Cerebral Palsy

Football Team, and now has used his experience to encourage and assist young people through the Youth Trust.

I also had the opportunity to interview Alistair, who gracefully shared the following with me, as **YOU** read this interview, be sure to highlight the answers that resonate with you.

Me: *Thank you for your time today Alistair. As advised earlier, this book is a guide for those who are suffering early depression and stressful times.*

Q1) What were your thoughts when you first woke up and realised what had happened?

Alistair: *I couldn't quite believe it. My family filled me in on everything and there were days I couldn't see myself getting better, and somehow my family just got me through it.*

Me: *Yes I understand that. Having the right people is integral to have around you when recovering from any illness or operation.*

Q2) What do you think is the best trait that you have now, that you know you wouldn't have had you not experienced what you did?

Alistair: *To take time out and appreciate things (life in general).*

Me: *Q3) Why do you think the rate of early depression and rate of stress related illnesses has increased so dramatically of recent, and especially with younger generation?*

Alistair: *Fiona, I think it's because the media promotes unsustainable aspirations (that is perceived celebrity from having little to no achievement of moral value or significance) then when people see it's not as easy, they don't know how to take it.*

Me: *Q4) Name 3 things that you believe got you through that experience*

Alistair: *My family, my mindset, my physical strength although I do get back to the gym, I was a regular gym goer*

Me: *Q6) Name 7 things you are grateful and thankful for today.*

Alistair: *Don't have 7. I probably do and also I'm a simple man, my family and close friends and our health.*

Me: *Q7) OK, what was the one piece of advice that you consider really kept you going when you realised you weren't going to play football at the same level ever again?*

Alistair: *I struggled with it. My psychologist was the one who said to me, I would never be the same person again and work on being the person I was becoming now.*

ME: *Yes that also makes sense to me.*

It's my personal belief that when you are blessed to be successful in your career that you love, that career or calling and the lifestyle that accompanies it unknowingly almost can and does often become your identity.

When that identity is taken away so unexpectedly, it is a shock isn't it?

Alistair: *Exactly! Now though I'm doing things I never would have done had I not gone through what I did. My family and the medical professionals were fantastic to me and the Football Association also but it took time.*

ME: *Final question, if you had to encourage someone at the start of their recovery journey and or provide a quote to remember, what would you tell them, and why?*

Alistair: **BELIEVE! BELIEVE! BELIEVE!**
No matter whether you can see the light at the time, just know it's there!

Me: *Thank you for your time Alistair*

As advised by Alistair and his team, if you want to know more details about Alistair, then please do look him up on: Twitter account @aph_inspired

*What can you learn from his story?

1. Write down below 5 things that you may do differently now as a result of learning about Alistair's story.

_____
_____
_____
_____
_____

2. How would you have reacted in his place, prior to reading the interview? Be honest with yourself.

_____
_____
_____
_____
_____

3. How can you apply the 5 things you have written as your lessons you learnt from Alistair's story, into your own life, starting from today?

_____
_____
_____
_____
_____
_____
_____
_____

"

Believe in yourself. You are braver than you think, more talented than you know, and capable of more than you imagine.

Roy T. Bennett

"

CHAPTER SIX
GOD TURNED IT AROUND FOR GOOD

GOD TURNED IT AROUND FOR GOOD FOR HER - even if you don't believe in a higher power, may you still benefit from this woman's words?

People have been known at extreme times, when human effort alone is not enough, to come to understand spirituality in a way that is unique to them. Whether that is GOD or the Universe or Buddha or Allah or a different higher power, it is having the faith that things can and will get better.

The next lady I am grateful and thankful to have interviewed is Chrissy B. Her story is one that gives all Glory to GOD, which is both myself and Alistair's belief also.

As mentioned, all beliefs are personal and as such not discussed further in this book.

Me: *Chrissy, I know from reading the information on your website, that you were in fact suffering mainly anxiety and depression as a child and well into your teenage years and no one knew anything.*

Many of the readers would be able to align with this. Could you share what 3 things did you do to help recover?

Chrissy B: *I never ever lost hope that my life could change - even through the darkest moments, something deep inside was telling me that my life wasn't meant to be that way. I held on to that or else I don't know what would have happened to me if I hadn't.*
.

Me: *Yes Hope is really what it is all about. One of my favourite quotes from Nick Vujicic is he was never really crippled until he lost hope. This is from a man born without arms or legs! Chrissy, what do you think was the MOST important thing you did that really made the difference in your recovery?*

Chrissy: *I started to stand up to depression and fight back. I developed a personal relationship with God and since then, my life has never been the same. I don't "manage" depression. I got rid of it completely. I've not had a relapse for over 20 years of any of the issues I had, and I never will.*

My relationship with God keeps me strong and I have a very positive attitude. Even when I encounter problems, I try to look at things in a logical way, rather than an emotional one.

I think more rather than give in to the feelings that try to come. This enables me to overcome any obstacles.

Thanks so much!

Again, looking at the answers and Chrissy's story, how can you relate this to your life?

Whether it's depression, diabetes, in some people cases that are blessed to recover it could be even cancer. All the diseases of the world are trying to tell us, the DIS- EASE that our bodies are experiencing because our life has got out of balance in some way.

"
Hardships often prepare ordinary people for an extraordinary destiny.

C.S. Lewis

"

CHAPTER SEVEN
LAUGHTER IS THE BEST MEDICINE

In this chapter we will be discussing the following topics:

*What is Gelotology?
*Brain Facts
*How does laughter really help us?

***What is Gelotology?**

If you were to check the Cambridge English dictionary, you would see under the definition of "laughter is the best medicine" it would say-

> **"Trying to be happy is a good way to stop worrying."**

In other words, it means that despite all else that may be going on, often laughter is a good way to help cure any negative feelings such as stress, worry or anger.

Can this actually be proved though?
The answer is YES!
There are people that have dedicated their life purpose to this cause. They are known as Geologists and the study of the effect laughing has on our brains is called Geolotology.

***Brain Facts:**

It may seem unusual that people could study the effect of laughter on the brain, however when we look at how the different areas of our brains function and what actually happens when we laugh, it's actually in my personal belief, quite amazing.

Following is a diagram of a brain with all the different areas labelled accordingly.

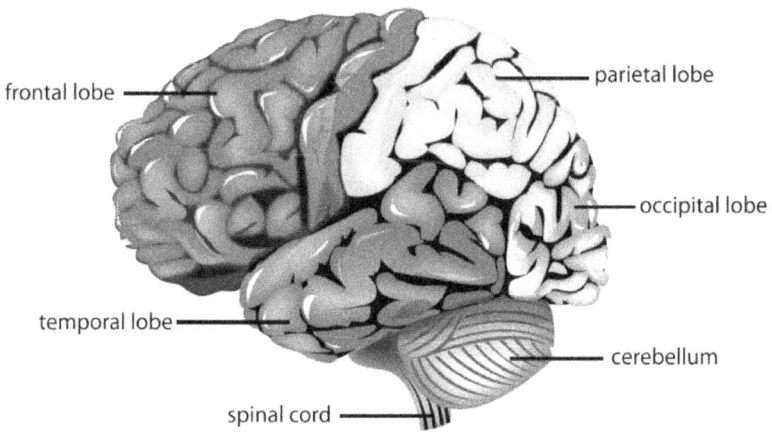

(This diagram was obtained from Vectorstock)

Our brain consists of:

- ✓ **Frontal Lobe**

The frontal lobe is involved in a person's motor skills functioning, enables problem solving, and also involved in working to ensure a person memory, language, judgement, social and sexual behaviour is all at its peak.

- ✓ **Temporal Lobe**

Responsible for processing auditory information from the ears. The temporal lobe mainly revolves around hearing and also selective listening.

- ✓ **Brainstem/Spinal cord**

The brain stem controls the flow of messages between the brain and the rest of the body. It also controls basic body functions such as breathing, swallowing, heart rate, blood pressure, consciousness and whether one is awake or sleepy.

- ✓ **Cerebellum**

The cerebellum coordinates voluntary movements such as posture, balance, coordination and speech, resulting in smooth and balanced muscular activity.

- ✓ **Occipital Lobes**

The occipital lobes are responsible for what your eyes see. They have to be extremely quick to process the large volume of information.

- ✓ **Prefrontal Cortex**

Which is the part of the brain located at the front of the frontal lobe. It greatly contributes to personality development. This part processes feelings of empathy, shame, compassion and guilt.

There are other parts to our brains however for the purposes of this chapter I have only concentrated on the main areas as mentioned.

When we laugh, it allows endorphins (those happy hormones) to be released and creates the natural feel good chemicals in our body as spoken about in Chapter 3 and stimulates different parts of our brain.

It is also beneficial to other parts of our body, such as;

OUR HEART

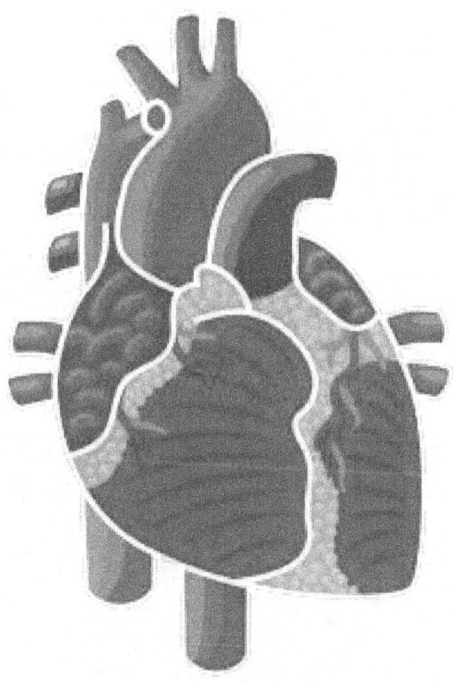

(Image obtained from 'Heart schematic human organs, Human Body, Clipart)

OUR LUNGS

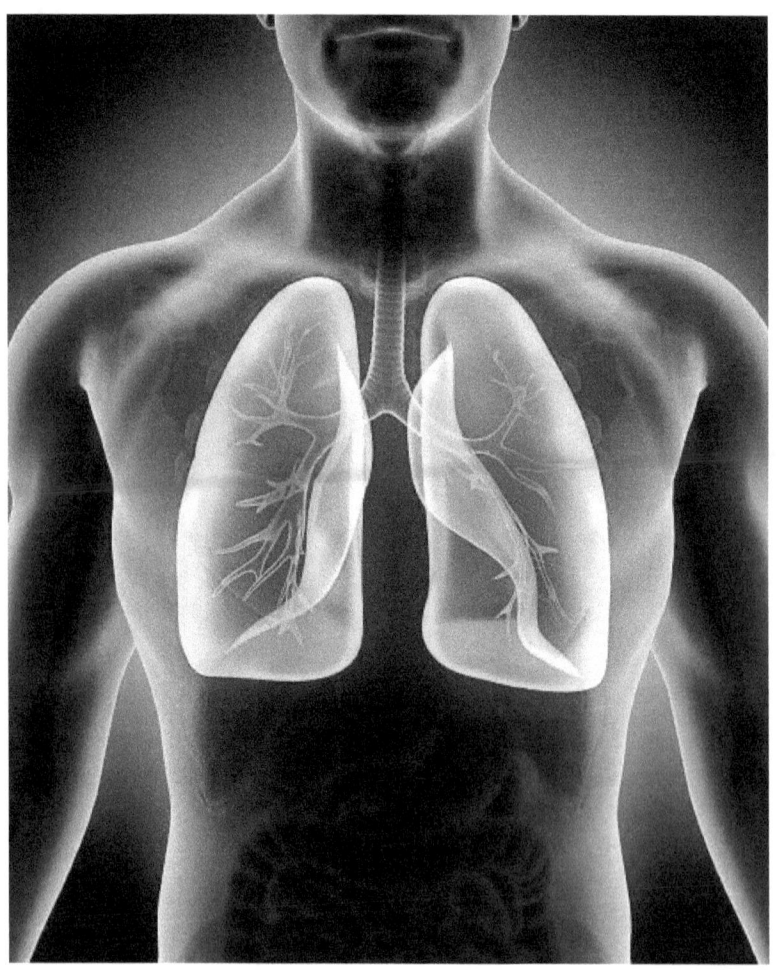

(Image obtained from 'Royalty Free Human Lung Pictures, Images and Stock Photos – iStock)

OUR MUSCLES

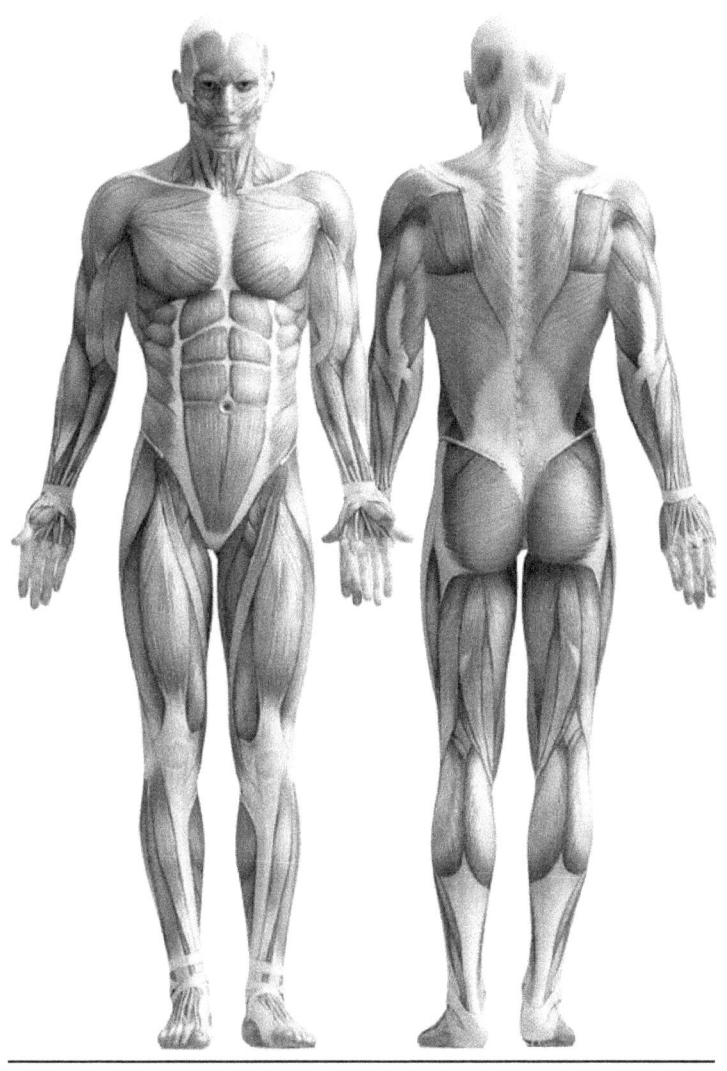

(Image of the muscles obtained from 'Muscles body muscles of the body free - digikalla.info')

Yes that's right, were you aware that when you release a hearty laugh, your muscles are also benefitting!

The muscles in your stomach expand and contract similarly to when you exercise your abdominal muscles.

Although laughing is good for us, please be mindful, too much can also work the opposite. All in moderation is usually a good way of thinking of things.

Given the nature of the book, other than for disclaimer purposes, no more regarding the negative consequences will be discussed.

Instead, I'm also extremely grateful to another good friend of mine, David Wilkes whose details can be found at the start of this book for sharing really what laughter is about.

LAUGHTER

In this beautiful world of ours you don't have to
have an exquisite supernatural character to be blessed
with laughter

Go ahead it's within you just try
It's a lot happier than the opposite which is to cry
It's within you and it's within me it's within everyone
In fact I tried it recently
Go ahead its so much fun

They say laughter keeps you younger
This is what the researchers are seeing
In fact it has so many benefits
It's a great contribution to your well-being

So be it a hearty belly laugh or a cheeky one
Let some laughter have a positive impact on your life
For genuine laughter with family and friends can
create happy memories and great enjoyable times

Copyright David Wilkes 2018

"

Success is not final, failure is not fatal: it is the courage to continue that counts.

Winston Churchill

"

CHAPTER EIGHT
OXYGEN AND OBSERVE

In this chapter we will be discussing about the following topics:

*How fast is too fast?
*Bask in YOUR breathing space?
*What else can I do?

***How fast is too fast?**

In our society today, people are being encouraged more and more to hustle daily to be able to reach their goals.

How often have you heard the expression, the "early bird gets the early worm?"

This hustling is OK when you are at optimum health, however for benefit of recovery, to push yourself too much too quickly before your body is ready may actually only result in falling back which leads to further frustration, which then may release wrong adrenalin in your brain and so your recovery may be further delayed.

As your mental wellness and physical strength returns, you can slowly rebuild again

Just be aware that as shared throughout this book, recovery takes time and how long that time is, no one can say. It's different for everyone. Just know that you really do have to keep on keeping on

You are worth it, even if you don't see it now. I know it's possible, so I encourage you, just keep doing the right behaviours daily and one day, you will see that you have evolved into a different person, that can also go on to really help others, if you choose to.

*Bask in your breathing space?

Circle below, where you feel most relaxed?

A) Quiet room away from your house,

B) Outside amongst nature,

C) My Car,

D) My bedroom

E) A room in your house?

Whichever place you have circled above, do make a conscious appointment with yourself daily to visit that place for **minimum 30 minutes every day and while there, and just be present. Take that time to not**

think of anything other than you fully recovered and make new plans for how you will live life.

Some of you may be thinking, what does it mean to be present?

All that means simply is to allow yourself to take note of your space and while you are there in such a way that you engage all of your 5 senses,

Think about:
What you hear?
What you see?
What can you feel when you are in your breathing space?
Are there any particular scents to the air/room you are in?

Observe what is happening around you in such great detail.

If you are unable to physically leave your premises, then simply breathing slower and maybe doing a puzzle or art can also help.

***What else can I do?**

Other examples of popular activities to take up at this time, if you do find yourself needing to slow down for a time, while you focus on recovery is to:

*Pick up yoga,

* Take a daily walk in nature,

*Allow yourself to only watch and listen to positive messages on YouTube, TV and or social media.

*Listen to classical music or any music of your choice that allows you to feel good.

*Volunteer your time at a local charity or school. Taking the onus off you and helping someone else is also beneficial to your wellbeing when you aren't at your optimum health as yet.

So even though it's true the early bird gets the worm, its also true to remind yourself that while you are where you are right now, listen to your body when it's trying to tell you its time to change your lifestyle for a period of time.

> All our dreams can come true, if we have the courage to pursue them.
>
> Walt Disney

CHAPTER NINE

SLEEPING SOUNDLY

In this chapter we will be discussing about the following topics:

*How Harmful is sleep Deprivation
*What difference could a sleep routine make?
*Quirky Sleep Facts

*How harmful is sleep deprivation?

Did you know that one of the most effective interrogation techniques used in other countries is sleep deprivation?

Why?

This is because sleep deprivation (extreme lack of sleep) attacks the biological functions at the core of your mental and physical health. This lack of sleep literally damages your brain cells!

If you are someone who finds it a challenge to fall asleep even when you are tired, and find yourself overthinking when it's time for bed, it's time to put in a routine.

WHAT DIFFERENCE CAN A SLEEP ROUTINE MAKE?

Having a routine of any kind helps you. It can alleviate stress which means less anxiety and certainly your mental health will thank you for it.

It's not any different for sleep. A bedtime routine subconsciously prepares you for a good night sleep.

This routine could include having a warm bath before bed, having a hot drink directly before going to bed or you could even include the following superfoods (refer back to chapter 3) in your diet, that will help you sleep such as;

- Almonds.
- Chamomile Tea.
- Cherry Juice.

It is important also to get into a habit of learning to switch off your laptop and keep your phone away from you.

This also helps in the morning because it encourages you to get out of bed to reach your phone anyway.

Why do you have to switch off your laptop and phone even in today's society switching off the phone isn't easy?

It's been proven that having your phone and other technological items near you when sleeping can disturb your sleep because even when turned off, these items still give off radiation waves that interrupt your sleep.

QUIRKY SLEEP FACTS

1. Sexomania exists! In earlier chapter we spoke about the endorphin release when having sex. Well, some people are known to have sex in their sleep, this isn't as uncommon as people may think.
So for all you consenting adults out there, a good reason to get into a sleep routine.

2. Generally speaking, most healthy adults need seven to nine hours of sleep a night.
However, saying this as with most things it depends on the individual because some individuals are able to function without sleepiness or drowsiness after as little as five to

six hours while others as they get older need their full ten hours sleep.

3. We are the only mammals that can actually delay our sleep.

4. Some people are actually known to be able to fall asleep with their eyes open (obtained from Quora, I wanted to check if it was possible and share with you the reader)! However as you can imagine their eyes would be red and irritated when they wake up.

5. Some people dream in colour while others dream in black and white. Apparently we dream every night, even if we don't remember it the next day.

"

Our greatest glory is not in never falling, but in rising every time we fall.

Confucius

"

CHAPTER TEN

NOW OVER TO YOU....

This final chapter is now over to you.

So now that you know the following in brief:

- Your attitude will ALWAYS determine your altitude
- You have greatness in YOU
- Animals really can be a humans best friend
- We have happy chemicals in our body that can make us feel good.
- Superfoods can make us feel super
- Others experiences can teach us much if we but let them
- Laughter is important in life
- Breathing techniques are extremely effective
- Beauty sleep not only affects our appearance it also affects our brains.
- Mindset is everything

The final exercises are to look back at your chart in chapter one, and think of how you can start to work on improving your scores even more right now as you work towards your recovery.

Who are the people you can enlist to help you?

Invest in a journal and write daily how you feel if no one else is around.

And finally, the last exercise is despite everything you may feel right now, I want you to start waking up every day and think of 3 things you are really glad you have going for you in your life.

It could be just waking up and seeing family, friends whether they come to visit you or you are able to visit them.

It could be just knowing people love you. It could be a variety of things. Whatever means a lot to you!

Keep working on this GRATITUDE ATTITUDE as much as all the other steps in this book.

I pray that over time, you too will find that recovery is possible. You learn to not only find however to also learn to love that better version of yourself evolving and go on to find out like Alistair said, even though you may not see the light right now, know that is there. And as Chrissy B said trust in God/ your higher power.

"

Gratitude unlocks the fullness of life. It turns what we have into enough, and more. It turns denial into acceptance, chaos to order, confusion to clarity. It can turn a meal into a feast, a house into a home, a stranger into a friend.

Melody Beattie

"

EPILOGUE

Finally, thank you for purchasing this book. Every subject discussed is shown in more detail in our workshops.

For details and to contact with Seigneur Strategies directly, please feel free to connect on:

Facebook: https://www.facebook.com/fionaseigneur

Instagram: https://www.instagram.com/fionaseigneur

Twitter: https://twitter.com/fionaseigneur

LinkedIn: https:// Fiona.seigneur

Love and Blessings of the most beautiful kind.

ALL TOPICS CONTAINED IN THIS BOOK ARE COVERED IN MORE DETAIL IN OUR SEIGNEUR STRATEGIES PACKAGES, MORE DETAILS CAN BE FOUND ON THE WEBSITE AT:

www.seigneurstrategies.com (still in progress at time of publishing this book)

ABOUT THE AUTHOR

Fiona worked in the Corporate Banking Sector for many years before she surrendered to her passion in writing and taking up Public Speaking and Coaching others in improving all aspects of their Wellbeing. Although this is her first book, it is one in a series entitled "HONORING YOU" that she is still in the process of sending to print.

Each book has the same style chapters and all is written to inspire future generations, how to ensure that all aspects of their wellbeing are looked after, from their health to their finances and relationships and everything in between.

"

We May Encounter Many Defeats but We Must Not Be Defeated

Maya Angelou

"

Direction

This personalised poem,
somewhere must get a mention,
simply I've named it... direction .

In life people don't plan to fail
they only fail to plan, in life all you can do,
is the best that you can.

Stay focused, continue to try, try, try
and as soon as you wake up,
you must lift your head up high.

On your journey,
if it doesn't feel right, then keep left
and follow roads where many successful people have
stepped.

Go forward for ever, in your precious life,
going backwards isn't an option,
I don't want to say this twice.

Believe in yourself
you'll be in for a pleasant surprise,
stay positive and
keep your eyes, firmly on the prize.

Feed your brain with healthy food,
at breakfast, lunch and dinner and
in your personal world tell yourself,
there's only one winner.

By Dave Wilkes

© copyrights Dave Wilkes 2016

www.ingramcontent.com/pod-product-compliance
Lightning Source LLC
LaVergne TN
LVHW051657080426
835511LV00017B/2613